ANIMAL WORLD

THE WEIRDEST ANIMALS IN THE WORLD

by Clara MacCarald

BrightPoint Press

San Diego, CA

© 2024 BrightPoint Press
an imprint of ReferencePoint Press, Inc.
Printed in the United States

For more information, contact:
BrightPoint Press
PO Box 27779
San Diego, CA 92198
www.BrightPointPress.com

ALL RIGHTS RESERVED.

No part of this work covered by the copyright hereon may be reproduced or used in any form or by any means—graphic, electronic, or mechanical, including photocopying, recording, taping, web distribution, or information storage retrieval systems—without the written permission of the publisher.

LIBRARY OF CONGRESS CATALOGING-IN-PUBLICATION DATA

Names: MacCarald, Clara, 1979- author.
Title: The weirdest animals in the world / by Clara MacCarald.
Description: San Diego, CA: BrightPoint, [2024] | Series: Animal world | Includes bibliographical references and index. | Audience: Ages 13 | Audience: Grades 7-9
Identifiers: LCCN 2023012544 (print) | LCCN 2023012545 (eBook) | ISBN 9781678206208 (hardcover) | ISBN 9781678206215 (eBook)
Subjects: LCSH: Animals--Juvenile literature. | Animals--Miscellanea--Juvenile literature.
Classification: LCC QL49 .M15225 2024 (print) | LCC QL49 (eBook) | DDC 590.2--dc23/eng/20230315
LC record available at https://lccn.loc.gov/2023012544
LC eBook record available at https://lccn.loc.gov/2023012545

CONTENTS

AT A GLANCE	4
INTRODUCTION A SLIMY SUPERPOWER	6
CHAPTER ONE PLATYPUSES	12
CHAPTER TWO LEAFY SEA DRAGONS	24
CHAPTER THREE HAGFISH	34
CHAPTER FOUR AYE-AYES	46
Glossary	58
Source Notes	59
For Further Research	60
Index	62
Image Credits	63
About the Author	64

AT A GLANCE

- Some animals are weird. They may have odd features or strange ways of protecting themselves.

- Platypuses are mammals that live in Australia. They have no teeth and no stomach. Instead of chewing their prey with teeth, platypuses eat bits of gravel to help mash up their food.

- Female platypuses lay eggs and produce milk that seeps out of their skin. The females use their milk to feed their young.

- Leafy sea dragons look like floating bits of seaweed. They have leafy spines all over their bodies and can change color to match their surroundings.

- Leafy sea dragons use their strange appearance to camouflage in seaweed meadows. This helps them avoid predators.

- Hagfish have no bones and can tie themselves into knots. They can also make slime.

- When threatened, a hagfish will release its slime. The slime clogs its target's gills. This makes the predator choke and can save the hagfish from being eaten.

- Aye-ayes are primates that have teeth and skulls similar to those of rodents. Each aye-aye also has a long, bony finger on each hand.

- The aye-aye uses its long fingers to find grubs. It taps on logs and finds areas that sound hollow. Then it uses its rodent-like teeth to bite through the wood and find food.

INTRODUCTION

A SLIMY SUPERPOWER

A hungry seal shark swims just above the ocean floor. It's on the hunt for a tasty fish. It comes across the faint smell of blood. This might be just what the animal needs. The shark follows the smell, hoping for an easy meal.

A dead fish rests on the seabed. But the shark isn't the first animal on the scene. A hagfish is already eating the dead creature. The hagfish's long body ripples as it takes each bite.

Hagfish don't have eyes. They detect food with their great sense of smell.

Hagfish slime is 99.996 percent seawater.

The eellike hagfish looks like the perfect prey. No scales or spikes protect its wrinkled skin. It looks defenseless. In fact, the hagfish doesn't even seem to notice the predator's approach.

The shark darts in for the kill. It opens its mouth around the hagfish's body. It bites down. But before the shark breaks skin, slime shoots out of the hagfish and surrounds the shark's head.

Slime is the hagfish's secret weapon for protecting itself. The slime gets into the shark's gills. Choking, the shark lets go of the hagfish. The predator swims off in alarm. Slime hangs off of its body.

The hagfish returns to its meal. For other animals, hagfish slime is a weird and unwelcome surprise. For the hagfish, it's nothing out of the ordinary.

WEIRD ANIMALS

There are a lot of peculiar animals in the world. Some have an odd mix of features that seem to come from different kinds of animals. Other animals reproduce in unusual ways. Some may be missing common features, such as teeth or a stomach. Others have strange abilities, such as the hagfish's slime attack.

These animals may seem peculiar to humans. But the things that make them odd can be very important. They are often the things that help the animals survive.

Scientists estimate that 75 percent of all plant and animal species are undiscovered. There may be even more strange creatures that scientists don't know about.

1

PLATYPUSES

The platypus is one of the oddest animals on Earth. Platypuses have fur, a duck-like bill, and webbed feet. And that's just the start of their weirdness. Platypuses are **mammals** that lay eggs. Mother platypuses make milk that seeps out of their skin like sweat. Platypuses hunt by sensing electrical currents. Males have stingers on their back legs. They are strange creatures.

These peculiar animals live only in eastern Australia and on nearby islands. Platypuses eat **crustaceans** and other small water creatures. They live near streams, shallow lakes, and other bodies

Wild platypuses can live for more than twenty years.

of water. Adult males live alone. Females live alone except when they have young.

EGGS AND MILK

Almost all mammals give birth to live young. Platypuses are one of only a handful of mammals that lay eggs instead. The other egg-laying mammals are spiny creatures called echidnas. Platypus and echidna eggshells are soft and leathery like those of reptiles rather than hard like bird eggshells.

Female platypuses lay one to three eggs in a burrow. They curl themselves around the eggs to keep them warm. After about

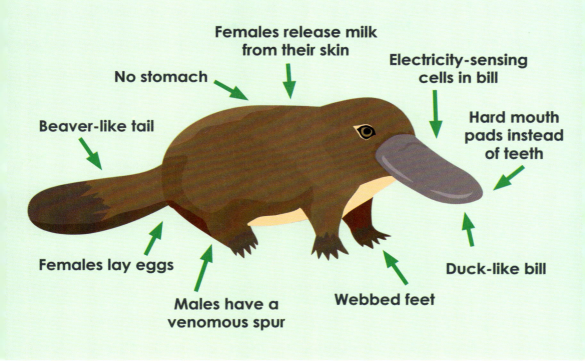

From its duck-like bill to its beaver-like tail, the platypus has a lot of weird features.

six to ten days, the babies hatch. The babies are tiny. Adult platypuses are on average around 20 inches (51 cm) from bill tip to tail. But newly hatched platypus

Baby platypuses are called puggles. Puggles depend on their mothers for food and protection until they're five months old.

babies are only about the size of a nickel.

They're completely helpless.

Like other mammals, platypus mothers feed their babies milk. The mothers don't have nipples, though. Nipples are the raised bits on female mammals that babies usually nurse from. Instead, platypus milk seeps out of the mother's skin.

ADAPTED FOR WATER

Platypuses have a difficult time walking on land. Their legs are short and stick out to the sides. Swimming is much easier for them. It takes a few months for a baby platypus to learn to swim. When a platypus swims, it paddles with its front feet. It uses its big flat tail and back feet to steer.

Underwater, a platypus closes its ears, eyes, and nose. This means the animal

Platypuses eat shellfish, insects, and worms.

can't hear, see, or smell while swimming. Fortunately, platypus bills can sense touch and sound waves. Platypus bills can also sense movement. Each bill has about 40,000 special cells for detecting electrical currents. Small animals make weak electrical currents as they move. Platypuses use these electrical currents to find prey.

The platypus doesn't have teeth to chew its prey with. Instead, its bill has hard pads inside. The platypus chews by eating gravel. It uses the gravel along with its hard pads to mash up its meal. Another common body part that the platypus is missing is a stomach. Once the platypus swallows, the food travels straight into a series of tubes called intestines that digest the food.

THREATS TO PLATYPUSES

Many predators prey on platypuses, especially on land. Native predators include eagles, dingoes, Tasmanian devils, and crocodiles. Red foxes, dogs, and cats also eat platypuses. These three predators are not native. People brought them to Australia.

Male platypuses have a special way of defending themselves from danger. They have stingers called spurs on their back ankles. The spurs can jab **venom** into another animal. Platypus venom is painful to people, but it can be deadly to other animals. Scientists think platypus males usually use the venom on each other rather than on predators. Males use it to paralyze each other during fights for mates.

Platypuses are not endangered yet, but their population is decreasing.

Australian law bans people from hunting platypuses. However, this doesn't mean these weird animals are safe. People still harm platypus **habitats**. If people take too much water out of streams, there's not enough left for platypuses. Pollution is another danger. Platypuses can get caught in fishing nets and drown.

Dams are another danger that platypuses face. In 2022, a study looked at platypus populations in areas with dams compared with areas without dams. "We knew the dams were a problem," says scientist Luis Mijangos, "but we didn't know how much

REAL OR FAKE?

In the 1800s, some people tried to fool others with fake creatures. For example, some people sewed fish tails onto the dead bodies of apes. They said the creatures were mermaids. When a preserved platypus was shipped from Australia, some English scientists thought it was another fake. They thought someone had sewn a duck's bill onto a mammal.

of a problem."[1] The study showed that the dams kept individual platypuses from traveling between habitats.

This is bad news for the **species**. If platypuses can't travel between habitats, then they can breed only with nearby platypuses. Groups of animals in which only a few individuals breed together are not as healthy as larger groups with many breeding individuals. The scientists in the study thought dams could explain why some platypus populations are shrinking. Fortunately, these weird and unique animals are still common in many places in Australia.

2
LEAFY SEA DRAGONS

Sea dragons are a type of fish. The leafy sea dragon is one of three sea dragon species. The leafy species is found off the southern and western coasts of Australia. It lives in rocky reefs and seaweed meadows. People sometimes call leafy sea dragons *leafies*.

A leafy sea dragon's backbone is oddly curved and bent. Its eyes can look in two different directions at once. A leafy sea dragon can be green, yellow, or brown. It has stripes on its body and marks on its spines. It can reach almost 18 inches (46 cm) in length.

Wild leafy sea dragons live up to nine years.

The leafy sea dragon's body is covered in hard plates. It's also covered from head to tail in spines. Some of the spines are sharp. These features protect the creature from predators. However, its best protection is its **camouflage**. The sea dragon's spines resemble leaves and stems of seaweed. This helps it hide from predators. It can even change color to improve its disguise.

THE LIFE OF A LEAFY

Leafy sea dragons swim using their leaflike fins. They use their tails and the fins on their necks to steer. However, sometimes they don't move at all. Leafy sea dragons will drift for days without moving. They eat while they float through the water. They suck their prey up through their tubelike snouts.

Even without teeth or a stomach, the leafy sea dragon has a big appetite. A single sea dragon must eat thousands of little

THE SEA DRAGON FAMILY

Weedy sea dragons and ruby sea dragons make up the rest of the sea dragon family. Weedy sea dragons are about 18 inches (46 cm) long. They have reddish bodies with spines and fewer leafy bits than their leafy sea dragon cousins. They live off the coasts of Tasmania and Australia. Ruby sea dragons weren't discovered until 2015. The species looks like weedy sea dragons, but it has a more vibrant red color. Ruby sea dragons live near Western Australia.

Sea dragons live alone. They seek out other sea dragons only when it's time to breed.

creatures every day. Its diet includes tiny crustaceans, **plankton**, and baby fish.

At about 1 to 2 years of age, sea dragons are able to have babies. A male sea dragon courts a female by dancing with her at sunset. The two sea dragons mirror each other's movements as they dance. Adam Chapman helped make a video of sea dragons dancing. "It is so beautiful and graceful," he says. "There is no sense that they are at all concerned about anything other than each other."[2]

At the end of the dance, the female sea dragon produces about 250 pink eggs. She lays the eggs on a special patch under the male's tail. The male provides the eggs with oxygen. After a few weeks, the eggs hatch. The babies are on their own.

LEAFY SEA DRAGON POPULATIONS

People once took many leafy sea dragons out of the wild. Divers liked how the creatures looked. They wanted to keep the animals as pets. But it's difficult to take care of leafy sea dragons. It's hard to keep them alive in a tank. Leafy sea dragons are also very difficult to breed in captivity.

WACKY RELATIVES

Sea dragons are related to seahorses and pipefish. There are about fifty species of seahorses and more than 200 species of pipefish. These species have a lot in common with sea dragons. None of the animals have teeth, they all have long snouts that suck up prey, and the males are the ones that carry the eggs.

Though leafy sea dragons are protected by Australian law, poachers capture the animals to sell as pets.

Rain washes fertilizers into the ocean, polluting the kelp forests where sea dragons live.

In the early 1990s, the Australian government worried that wild leafy sea dragon populations were too low. The government passed laws to protect the species. Now, only one pregnant sea dragon is captured each year. The babies are hatched in captivity and given to zoos and aquariums to be used for education and science.

Leafy sea dragons still face threats today. The animals swim very slowly and don't travel far. They can die if they get trapped in nets. Their habitats are also in danger. Waste from human cities has harmed the reefs and seagrass beds where the sea dragons live. Scientists think that sea dragon populations might be dropping. But for now, this weird species continues to survive.

3

HAGFISH

Some people call hagfish slime eels. But they are not closely related to eels, and they are a lot stranger than just being slimy fish. The things hagfish lack are almost as weird as the features they have. Hagfish have no jaw, no bones, no scales, no eyes, and only one nose hole. They're so strange that it took scientists a long time even to decide that hagfish are fish.

There are seventy-six species of hagfish around the world. Most hagfish are about 1 foot (0.3 m) long. One species grows more than 4 feet (1.2 m) long.

Atlantic hagfish use their sharp teeth to hunt crustaceans and worms.

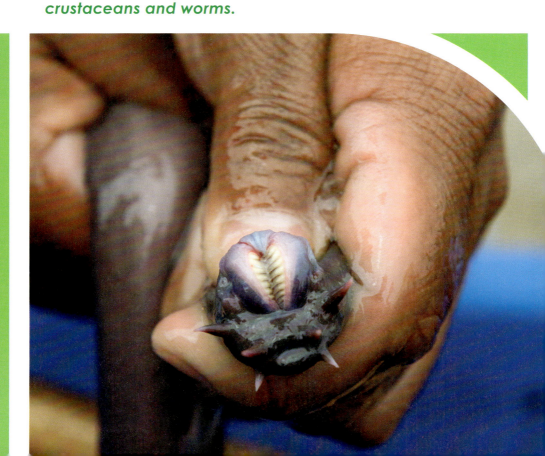

Some hagfish hunt. But often they eat animals that are already dead.

INSIDE A HAGFISH

Hagfish are one of only two kinds of fish without a jaw. The other is the lamprey. Although hagfish have no jaw or bones, they do have a skull. The skull is made of cartilage. Cartilage is a type of body tissue. It bends more easily than bone and feels a bit like plastic. Cartilage is what gives human noses and ears their shape.

Hagfish don't have true eyes. Instead, they have eye spots. Some hagfish species

Hagfish hide during the day and hunt at night.

can use their eye spots to sense light. Other species have eye spots that are blocked by skin and muscle.

Hagfish have weird mouths too. They have two rows of unusual teeth. The teeth are made of keratin. This is the same material that makes up animal hair and horns. Hagfish also have fleshy bits around their mouths called barbels. Each hagfish has six to eight barbels. The barbels help hagfish navigate and find food.

HUNGRY HAGFISH

Hagfish eat mostly animals that are already dead. Scientist Douglas Fudge says, "When something dead falls to the bottom of the ocean, it's usually a hagfish that gets there first."[3] If the dead animal is large, the hagfish burrows inside the body. It then eats the animal from the inside out.

While hagfish will eat many kinds of dead fish, few things can eat hagfish. Animals such as seabirds and seals that don't have gills have an easier time eating them, but they don't often bother. When it comes to finding a meal, hagfish are often more trouble than they are worth.

The hagfish's most famous feature is its slime. Hagfish will release slime when

SUPER SKIN

Hagfish can survive for months without feasting on dead fish. As they swim through the ocean, their skin absorbs nutrients in the water. This keeps them fed even when they can't find a large meal.

attacked. They also might release slime when a fish is trying to steal their food.

Inside hagfish are tightly wound threads of slime. The animals have pores on the sides of their bodies to let out the threads. When the slime hits seawater, the threads unwind rapidly. They tangle up with each other and gather water. It all swells into a big mass of soft slime. One hagfish can create a bucketful of slime in less than a second.

Slime sounds gross, but the slime the hagfish release isn't dirty. "You can pick it up in a glob, stretch it out in a sheet and drop it, and nothing will be on your skin,"

Doctors are researching using hagfish slime to bandage wounds and treat burns.

says scientist Aaron Baldwin. "It's clean slime."[4]

Hagfish slime can be deadly to fish. The slime can clog a predator's gills. Fish use

41

their gills to get oxygen. A fish covered in hagfish slime could suffocate. The slime is a danger to hagfish too. To get rid of it, the animals can sneeze it out of their noses. They can also free themselves with an interesting trick. Because the creatures have no bones, they're very flexible. When they get covered in slime, they tie themselves into a knot. As they slide out of the knot, they can scrape the slime off their bodies.

HAGFISH AND PEOPLE

Hagfish are a popular food in Korea. Koreans eat about 5 million pounds

Hagfish meat is often eaten grilled or barbecued. The slime can be used as an egg substitute.

(2.3 million kg) of hagfish every year. People also use hagfish skin to make leather.

Some people are interested in using hagfish slime to make things. The threads of hagfish slime are thin but very strong.

Nine species of hagfish are in danger of extinction. Overfishing is one threat to their populations.

People want to try manufacturing the slime into cloth. The US Navy is also considering using the slime to stop enemy ships.

Fishing is a threat to several hagfish species. People catch hagfish on purpose.

They also catch the animals accidentally while trying to catch other fish.

Despite being odd, hagfish are important to life in the ocean. They keep the ocean floor clean by eating dead fish. The oceans need these strange animals.

HAGFISH DAY

The third Wednesday in October is National Hagfish Day. The group WhaleTimes started Hagfish Day in 2009. It said it wanted to celebrate the "beauty of ugly." WhaleTimes also wanted to let people know that hagfish are important to the oceans. The organization suggests that people make slime to celebrate Hagfish Day.

"Hagfish Day!" WhaleTimes Inc., 2022. https://whaletimes.org.

4
AYE-AYES

The bushy-tailed aye-aye looks a bit like a cross between a squirrel and a possum. In fact, scientists once identified the animal as a kind of squirrel. Scientists now know that aye-ayes are **primates**.

Aye-ayes have big ears and big eyes. They have flat faces and tails longer than their bodies. But an aye-aye's weirdest features are its hands. Each hand has six digits. The third finger is bonelike and very long.

Most aye-ayes live in the rain forests of Madagascar. Madagascar is a large island

Wild aye-ayes can live for twenty years.

off the eastern coast of Africa. Aye-ayes live alone. They live in trees, eating insects and fruit. Aye-ayes are endangered. This means the species is at risk of dying out. The animal's odd looks may be one reason the primates are in trouble.

A STRANGE PRIMATE

Primates all share a few features. They have large brains compared with similar-sized animals. Their eyes face forward. Having forward-facing eyes helps animals judge distances. This is a useful skill for primates that move around in trees. Aye-ayes belong

The average aye-aye weighs between 5 and 6 pounds (2.3–2.7 kg).

to a group of primates called lemurs. Most other lemurs also live in Madagascar.

Aye-ayes are active mostly at night. They use their big eyes to see in the dark.

Aye-ayes are the largest nocturnal primates. When afraid, aye-ayes can puff out their fur to look bigger.

Aye-ayes have very strange teeth. Some of their front teeth are always growing. Teeth that keep growing are a feature of rodents, not primates. An aye-aye's skull also resembles that of a rodent. "The shape of the skull is what makes the aye-aye look so similar to squirrels," says scientist Philip Cox.[5]

Cox was part of a study that compared the heads of the two species. Squirrels use their teeth and jaws to crack nuts. The teeth

Aye-ayes are preyed on by large birds and catlike creatures called fossas.

and jaws of aye-ayes are very strong too. In zoos, the animals can bite through concrete walls. Cox and his team found that wild

Aye-ayes eat fruit such as bananas, coconuts, lychees, mangoes, and more.

aye-ayes need such strong teeth to bite through trees. Aye-ayes use this ability to find grubs. Grubs are insect larvae.

AN UNUSUAL FINGER

To find grubs, aye-ayes use echolocation. Echolocation is the use of sound to locate things. Aye-ayes are the only primates that echolocate.

To find food, an aye-aye taps its thin, bony finger on the bark of trees and logs. The primate's big ears listen closely to the sound. It listens for hollow areas. The hollow areas are made when grubs chew through the wood. When tapped, hollow areas sound different from solid areas.

Once the aye-aye finds its prey, it chews an opening in the wood. Then it sticks its long finger inside. The finger can swivel in every direction. The aye-aye snags the grub with a claw and eats it. It can also use its weird finger to scoop out and eat fruit pulp.

Scientists have seen aye-ayes use their long fingers to dig for something else: snot. Aye-ayes pick their own noses and eat what they find. "I was really surprised to

NOSEPICKERS

Besides aye-ayes, at least eleven other primates pick their noses. These species include chimps, gorillas, and monkeys. Primates use their fingers to pick their noses. They can also use tools such as sticks. Other mammals pick their noses too. Giraffes can stick their long tongues in their noses to clean out snot.

see this," says scientist Anne-Claire Fabre. Fabre led a research study looking into the nose-picking behavior. "To fit the entirety of its third finger into its nose is pretty impressive!" she says.[6] An aye-aye's finger can reach all the way through its nose and into its throat.

AYE-AYES AND HUMANS

Aye-aye populations have been decreasing since the 1980s. One threat to aye-ayes is hunting by humans. Some people kill ayes-ayes to eat them. Others kill them out of fear. They think aye-ayes bring bad luck.

People tell different stories about aye-ayes. Some say an aye-aye can cast a curse by pointing its bony finger at someone. Others say the finger is used to dig out human hearts.

The biggest threat to aye-ayes is the loss of their forest habitats. From 1973 to 2014, people cut down more than one-third of Madagascar's forests. Scientists are working to better understand aye-ayes' needs. They are hoping to make sure the world doesn't lose this peculiar creature.

Some animals are pretty weird. Some have features that might even seem

Scientists estimate that only 1,000 to 10,000 aye-ayes are left in the world.

unbelievable. But the weird creatures of the world are also very interesting. They are important parts of life on Earth.

GLOSSARY

camouflage

features that hide an animal by blending it into its surroundings

crustaceans

animals with hard outsides and no backbones, such as crabs and shrimp

habitats

the places where a plant or an animal lives

mammals

individuals in a class of warm-blooded animals that have hair or fur and produce milk to feed their young

plankton

small organisms that live in water, including tiny animals and plants

primates

a group of related animals that include monkeys, apes, and humans

species

a closely related group of living things that can produce fertile young

venom

a poison that animals put into other animals through biting or stinging

SOURCE NOTES

CHAPTER ONE: PLATYPUSES

1. Quoted in Nicholas Bakalar, "Platypuses Face a Damned, Inbred Future," *New York Times*, November 4, 2022. www.nytimes.com.

CHAPTER TWO: LEAFY SEA DRAGONS

2. Quoted in Matt Walker, "Ghostly 'Dance of a Seadragon,'" *BBC Earth News*, October 29, 2009. https://news.bbc.co.uk.

CHAPTER THREE: HAGFISH

3. Quoted in Christine Dell'Amore, "Seven Reasons Hagfish Are Amazing (#6: They Can Live in Dead Bodies)," *National Geographic*, March 10, 2017. www.nationalgeographic.com.

4. Quoted in Riley Woodford, "Hagfish Are Not Slime 'Eels': Biologists Investigate Amazing Sea Creature," *Alaska Fish & Wildlife News*, April 2018. https://adfg.alaska.gov.

CHAPTER FOUR: AYE-AYES

5. Quoted in Brooks Hays, "Aye-Aye's Strange Features Explained by New Study," *Science News*, August 1, 2018. www.upi.com.

6. Quoted in James Ashworth, "Aye-aye Recorded Picking Nose and Eating Snot for the First Time," *National History Museum*, October 27, 2022. www.nhm.ac.uk.

FOR FURTHER RESEARCH

BOOKS

Quinn M. Arnold, *Aye-Ayes*. Mankato, MN: Creative Education, 2019.

Sami Bayly, *A Curious Collection of Peculiar Creatures: An Illustrated Encyclopedia*. New York: The Experiment, 2020.

Nel Yomtov, *Strange Beasts*. North Mankato, MN: Capstone Press, 2021.

INTERNET SOURCES

"Aye-Aye," *Duke Lemur Center*, n.d. https://lemur.duke.edu.

"Platypus," *San Diego Zoo Wildlife Alliance*, n.d. https://animals.sandiegozoo.org.

"Wonder of the Day #978: Do Dragons Live in the Sea?" *Wonderopolis*, n.d. www.wonderopolis.org.

WEBSITES

DK Find Out!: Aye-Aye
www.dkfindout.com

DK Find Out! hosts articles and interactive activities about a wide variety of subjects. Its "Aye-Aye" page contains information about aye-ayes and links to related primates.

Monterey Bay Aquarium
www.montereybayaquarium.org

Monterey Bay Aquarium is located in Monterey, California. Its website has articles and live video feeds of many of its sea animals. The site has information about leafy sea dragons and hagfish.

World Wildlife Fund
www.worldwildlife.org

Founded in 1961, the World Wildlife Fund was created to protect Earth's wildlife. The organization works in nearly one hundred countries to save endangered species. Its website hosts information about platypuses, aye-ayes, and more.

INDEX

Africa, 48
Australia, 13, 20–21, 22, 23, 24, 27, 32
aye-ayes, 46–56

barbels, 38
bills, 12, 15, 18–19, 22

diets, 13, 27–28, 36, 38–39, 45, 48, 52–54

ears, 17, 46, 53
eggs, 12, 14–15, 29, 30
eyes, 17, 25, 34, 36–37, 46, 48, 49

feet, 12, 15, 17
fingers, 47, 53–56
fins, 26
fur, 12, 50

habitats, 13–14, 21, 23, 24, 27, 33, 47–48, 56
hagfish, 6–9, 10, 34–45
human activity, 20, 21–23, 30, 32–33, 42–45, 55–56

leafy sea dragons, 24–33
legs, 13, 17

Madagascar, 47, 49, 56

noses, 17, 27, 30, 34, 42, 54–55

platypuses, 12–23
predators, 6–9, 19–20, 26, 39–42

ruby sea dragons, 27

size, 15–16, 25, 27, 35
skin, 8–9, 12, 15, 17, 37, 39, 43
slime, 9, 10, 39–42, 43–44
spines, 25–26, 27
stingers, 13, 15, 20
stomachs, 10, 15, 19, 27

tail, 15, 17, 26, 29, 46–47
Tasmania, 27
teeth, 10, 15, 19, 27, 30, 37–38, 50–52

weedy sea dragons, 27

young, 14–17, 28–29

IMAGE CREDITS

Cover: © Michael Warwick/Shutterstock Images
5: © phototrip/iStockphoto
7: © NOAA Okeanos Explorer Program/NOAA
8: © ffennema/iStockphoto
11: © javarman3/iStockphoto
13: © slowmotiongli/iStockphoto
15: © artihart/Shutterstock Images
16: © Iain Stych/iStockphoto
18: © John Carnemolla/Shutterstock Images
21: © Michel Viard/iStockphoto
25: © Bonnie Taylor Barry/Shutterstock Images
28: © jwblinn/Shutterstock Images
31: © Kevin Ouellette/Shutterstock Images
32: © AshtonEa/iStockphoto
35: © Frank Fennema/Shutterstock Images
37: © NOAA Okeanos Explorer Program/NOAA
41: © Ronald Newsome/US Navy
43: © hyotographics/Shutterstock Images
44: © Bear Samurai/Shutterstock Images
47: © javarman/Shutterstock Images
49: © Michel Viard/iStockphoto
51: © dennisvdw/iStockphoto
52: © Ariadne Van Zandbergen/Alamy
57: © Homo Cosmicos/Shutterstock Images

ABOUT THE AUTHOR

Clara MacCarald is a freelance writer with a master's degree in ecology and natural resources. She lives with her family in an off-grid house nestled in the forests of central New York. When not parenting her daughter, she spends her time writing nonfiction books for kids.